IRVING BABBITT

AND

THE TEACHING OF LITERATURE

BY

Harry Levin

IRVING BABBITT PROFESSOR

OF COMPARATIVE LITERATURE

THIS lecture by Harry Levin was delivered in the Boylston Hall Auditorium, Harvard University, on Monday afternoon, November 7, 1960, to mark the inauguration of the new Irving Babbitt Professorship of Comparative Literature to which chair Mr. Levin was appointed earlier in the year. This chair honors the literary critic who was Professor of French Literature at Harvard from 1912 until his death in 1933 and a member of the teaching staff for nearly forty years. The professorship was established with funds given by Harvard alumni through the Program for Harvard College. An abbreviated version of this lecture has appeared in the *Harvard Alumni Bulletin*.

Himself a graduate of Harvard College, Professor Levin was a Junior Fellow of the Society of Fellows from 1934 to 1939, when he received his first teaching appointment at the University. He became Associate Professor of English in 1944 and Professor of English in 1948. From 1955 onward he held the title of Professor of English and of Comparative Literature. His volumes of literary criticism range over a wide variety of fields. Among them are *The Broken Column: A Study in Romantic Hellenism; James Joyce: A Critical Introduction; The Overreacher: A Study of Christopher Marlowe; Contexts of Criticism; The Power of Blackness: Hawthorne, Poe, Melville;* and *The Question of Hamlet*. Mr. Levin serves on the faculty committee for the new Loeb Drama Center, is a Senior Fellow of the Society of Fellows, and is chairman of the Division of Modern Languages.

WHEN James Russell Lowell was being persuaded to undertake the Smith Professorship of the French and Spanish Languages in 1855, Francis James Child held out to him "the privilege of free speech on the great themes of modern literature." Personally, I cannot imagine a more congenial privilege, especially when it is reinforced by the freedom of the Harvard College Library and the stimulus of an audience second to none in its avid concern for books and ideas. I am also poignantly aware that such incumbents as Lowell and Child himself, who relinquished the Boylston Professorship of Rhetoric and Oratory to become Harvard's first Professor of English in 1876, are no longer within calling distance; while, on the other hand, professorships have been proliferating through recent years, in accordance with trends of cultural inflation which have diffused and diluted college degrees, upgrading agricultural colleges into state universities and promoting freshmen from sections to seminars. As long ago as 1911, *The Nation*, committed in those days to hierarchical principles, ran an editorial proposing a "Super-Professorate." This was immediately countered by a sharply reasoned letter to the editor, questioning the criteria by which superprofessors were likely to be selected, and expressing a well grounded fear that intellectual discipline might count for less than enthusiastic popularization. The letter-writer, whose students could have recognized him even if he had not appended his signature, knew whereof he spoke. He was Irving Babbitt; he was then in his forty-sixth year; and he was still an Assistant Professor of French in Harvard University.

It was not until the following year, after he had been offered a post at a Middle Western university, that President Lowell named him as a Professor of French Literature. His colleague, the shrewd and assiduous J. D. M. Ford, though eight years younger than Babbitt, had been appointed to a full professorship five years before him. Whether this conspicuous neglect had been due to his forthright criticisms of President Eliot's policies, to the opposition of senior colleagues protecting a scholarly regimen which Babbitt had

3

already challenged, or to his own deliberate refusal to fall in with the requirements of the doctoral degree, it is now too late for speculation. But it is not surprising that he came to regard a faculty of arts and sciences as "an aggregate of mutually repellent particles" — perhaps, as such, a greater source of energy for him than it was for those who took a more static and self-satisfied view of it. What would our academic communities be if, in their continual process of reproducing themselves, they did not produce their monitors of dissent? How saliently the thought of Thorstein Veblen, who could not keep a professorial job, stands out from the dim apologetics of his conformable rivals! How necessary it must have been for our pioneering literary historian, V. L. Parrington, or for our leading Shakespearean commentator, E. E. Stoll — both of them disaffected Harvard alumni — to assume a controversial stance! What a loss for everyone when such productive tensions are cut short by protesting resignations, like those of Joel Elias Spingarn or Charles A. Beard from a sister institution!

Harvard has not been invulnerable to losses of that description. George Ticknor, despite his success in establishing the study of modern languages, felt balked in his further efforts here and resigned in mid-career. Little credit accrues to the University for its brief and marginal appointments of such brilliant figures as John Fiske and Charles Sanders Peirce. The self-searching chapter entitled "Failure" in *The Education of Henry Adams*, which deals with the autobiographer's seven-year assistant professorship, may well serve as a standing admonition to any member of our faculty who has managed to pass beyond that rank. And yet it was Henry Adams who proudly affirmed that "a teacher affects eternity; he can never tell where his influence stops." Babbitt's very resistance to current doctrines generated an apostolic zeal which indoctrinated a growing band of disciples. His pedagogical ascendancy, first asserted over his fellow graduate student, Paul Elmer More, naturally made most of its converts among younger teachers and future educators. However, in refutation of the later charge that Babbitt's influence stopped at the edge of the campus, if not of the Yard, it will not be forgotten that he was called master by our most eminent Anglo-

American man of letters. "To have once been a pupil of Babbitt's was to remain always in that position," T. S. Eliot has attested, "and to be grateful for (in my case) a very much qualified approval." Talented pupils were bound to diverge in their mature accomplishments; but "the magnitude of the debt" remained; and Van Wyck Brooks paused to acknowledge it parenthetically in his radical manifesto, *Letters and Leadership*.

The loyalties that Babbitt commanded — not to say pieties — may be gauged from the testimonial volume edited by Frederick T. Manchester and Odell Shepherd. Even more interesting would be the recollections of those who reacted from his teaching as divergently as Walter Lippmann, Gilbert Seldes, Crane Brinton, David McCord, Newton Arvin, Granville Hicks, Charles Wyzanski, David Riesman, and Ralph Kirkpatrick. Those who shrugged it off as merely parochial or anachronistic might have been surprised to come across some of its European affinities: with T. E. Hulme and Wyndham Lewis in England, with Charles Maurras and Julien Benda in France. Doctoral dissertations in various countries have been addressed to problems raised by this scholar who refused to write a thesis. His position, as he saw it, was less ambiguous than that of Charles W. Eliot, who represented the Puritan temperament at its best, and who had lent an air of respectability to the relaxation of educational standards. Hence it required a maverick to present the case for tradition, to wage a vehement polemic on behalf of the moderate virtues, to oppose a bland subversiveness with a cantankerous decorum, to campaign for restraint. Small wonder if Babbitt's intentions, so far as they had been bruited beyond the classroom, were misunderstood and resented. The precedent of Socrates had taught him that gadflies court disfavor, to say the least. At a time when the profession of letters stood farther apart from the halls of learning than it does today, he became a bugbear for the Bohemians, an advocate of the dead against the living, the arch-reactionary who comes out flatly against everything that matters. As irony would have it, his very surname — or rather, his homonym, used for a novel by Sinclair Lewis — became synonymous with philistine.

5

Latterly there have been signs to indicate that the reputation of Irving Babbitt might be emerging from its interval of eclipse. Though his cause seemed a losing one to his opponents, it is not yet lost a generation afterward. On the contrary, their causes — precisely because they seemed so up-to-date — have dated more than his old-fashioned values. If he dwelt in an ivory tower, it had windows which looked out and down on a clear and broad perspective. Thus he could warn international-minded readers against the futility of the League of Nations, the danger of uncontrolled military explosives, and "our growing unpopularity abroad." In 1924 he speculated:

Let us ask ourselves again whether the chances of a clash between America and Japan are likely to diminish if Japan becomes more democratic, if, in other words, the popular will is substituted for the will of a small group of "elder statesmen." Any one who knows what the Japanese sensational press has already done to foment suspicion against America is justified in harboring doubts on this point.

Back on the domestic front, as early as 1908, he had made this trenchant comment on the disparity between underprivileged citizens and predatory businessmen:

The eager efforts of our philanthropists to do something for the Negro and the newsboy are well enough in their way; but a society that hopes to be saved by what it does for its Negroes and its newsboys is a society that is trying to lift itself by its own boot-straps. Our real hope of safety lies in our being able to induce our future Harrimans and Rockefellers to liberalize their own souls, in other words to get themselves rightly educated.

Higher education was Babbitt's point of departure and point of return; on that ground his prophetic challenges were most fully justified and have been most squarely met. What he called "the Philological Syndicate" has been toppled by the sheer unbalanced poundage of its Germanized scholarship. Though the Ph.D. has not been abolished, it has been considerably humanized. Babbitt's plea for a teaching degree like the French agrégation, emphasizing wide reflection instead of narrow research, accords with the latest recommendations from our graduate deans. Meanwhile the decline of the classics seems, in Harvard at least, to have been shored. In 1925, Babbitt lamented, there were 12 graduate students in Ancient Languages to 216 in Modern; thirty-five years later, we have 37 in Ancient to 237 students in Modern Languages (excluding Radcliffe, where the respective enrollments have increased much more than proportionately). As for the colleges and their programs of undergraduate instruction, they have been inclining away from the lecture hall and toward the tutorial conference; General Education, with its core of great books, has moderated the chaos of free electives; and indeed there are some institutions where Aristotle rules with as heavy a hand as in the Middle Ages. Whether or not this reversion would have pleased Babbitt may be open to doubt. Citing Coleridge's remark that every man is either a Platonist or an Aristotelian, he used to add with characteristic pungency: "In my opinion, Coleridge was far too complimentary to the average man."

II

THE voice of reason that cried out so passionately in a wilderness of distractions had its retarded impact, which in turn has its fitting acknowledgment. "And thus the whirligig of time brings in his revenges." Since Babbitt was above all a teacher's teacher, his memorial takes a pedagogical form. One of his most devoted former pupils, as it so happily turns out, is presiding over our present era of development and revaluation at Harvard; and President Pusey has seen fit to mark Babbitt's contribution with a chair which will perpetuate his name. This recognition is double; for it not only honors a prophet within his own parish at last; it strengthens our relations with the larger Republic of Letters by sponsoring, as he unofficially did, the hopeful subject of Comparative Literature. At this point my professional enthusiasm is overtaken by my sense of personal limitation. The first incumbent of the Babbitt Professorship may boast of having been one of Professor Babbitt's last students; but "last" might also mean laggard in the pursuit of Babbitt's acquirements or hesitant in the acceptance of his tenets. Nor could

I claim a laying-on of hands without recalling a publication I have long tried to forget, a paper written originally for his course in Romanticism. When he heard that it would be published in a series of undergraduate essays — well, I will not do his memory the injustice of trying to quote him verbatim. His approval was qualified, of course, though he was generally encouraging and specifically helpful. I particularly remember the pensive statement that he himself had not published a book until well into his forties, along with the sobering query whether I was really old enough to practise as a critic.

I am now in a better position than I was then to appreciate the wisdom of such doubts, though I must add that they do not meet much agreement when I pass them on to my own students. The advantage that age exerts over youth is, at best, a temporary one; and it tends to decrease in a civilization which prides itself upon abridging all time-spans; yet the consequent advantage gained by youth is likewise, in its very nature, temporary. The cycle of generations regulates the habitual rhythms of education, insofar as humane learning must be accumulated before it can be imparted. Babbitt's preference for maturity was not a matter of calendar age or primarily of relative experience; it was a question of gaining a critic's license by getting to know one's business, so to speak, by mastering a complex and voluminous body of material. How could one judge or discriminate or generalize or trace relevant connections or, in short, make valid interpretations without such groundwork? Babbitt was, as detractors complained, an opinionated man; but no man ever took more pains to document his opinion. In effect, his teaching was premised upon the importance of holding definite opinions and — what is still more important — of earning the right to hold them through patient study and rigorous cogitation. Brash criticasters, bypassing those prerequisites, could — and do — arrive at quick and arresting conclusions; but Babbitt would have us examine their credentials before we mistake them for serious practitioners. Erudite scholars, at the other extreme, could be so overwhelmed by the tasks of accumulation and organization that they would all but abandon the hope of reaching any conclusion.

Babbitt, as usual, found the middle way more arduous than the extremes. With the curricular shift from ancient to modern languages, *litterae humaniores* had given place to philology; and philology, having made its linguistic and textual contributions, faced its point of diminishing returns. Lacking a direction of their own but influenced by the concurrent investigations of science, the philologists went on collecting and compiling with little regard for value or significance, and ended by subjecting the graduate schools to a pedantic cult of trivial detail. On the undergraduate level, the reaction to this esoteric professionalism was to make a classroom oracle of the literary dilettante, with his vague appreciations and studied mannerisms. Yet Babbitt, who had even less in common with a Copeland than with a Kittredge, impartially damned the feuding houses of impressionism and antiquarianism. Scholarship was the precondition of criticism, for him, as criticism was the consummation of scholarship. "The encyclopedia facts," as he regularly announced, were presupposed in his lectures and tested by his examinations. Repeatedly he reminded his listeners that "rounded estimates" of the works he cited would have had to put more stress upon their esthetic merits. But he frankly concentrated upon the transmission of ideas, and his pithy citations were carefully chosen to reveal the authors in their own phrases. Often the change of context introduced a harsher light; anything they had said, one suspected, might be held against them. However, the system was inclusive enough to be roughly equable in the long run. Everything that everyone had said was neatly filed away in some mental drawer, ready to be pulled out in response to some pertinent inquiry.

Babbitt the pedagogue is so vivid a ghost that I can never enter Sever 11 without envisioning that patriarchal white head, those Roman features, and those ponderous shoulders brooding over a desk he has just strewn with books in many languages. As he rustles through them, translating here and annotating there, his monologue becomes a dialogue in which the minds of all the ages participate. On a plane beneath his notice, it also became a lottery; for, during his sequence of quotations and references, he would mention between fifty and a hundred different names in the interim of a single hour; so that his more enterprising and less dedicated students could pool their pennies and draw lots for what might prove to be the final number, keeping check on the margins of their notebooks. Most of us, however, came to realize that we had a larger stake in the dialectical interplay. Mr. Babbitt's courses usually started with a *bibliographie raisonnée*, where the listed authorities came alive, and began to jostle for position, as soon as he had dictated their titles and dates. He proceeded, in Socratic fashion, by defining a series of basic terms: words providing the keys to fundamental concepts, retraced across the length and breadth of history through exhilarating semantic excursions. Frequently he brought his points home with topical allusions: timely newspaper clippings or public utterances, constituting a sort of *sottisier* or scrapbook of contemporary fatuities. But the farther he went back into the past, the wiser seemed the bywords with which he returned. His pedagogy admitted us to a pantheon of thinkers — classical, scriptural, scholastic, humanistic, oriental — whose views were canvassed, and messages conveyed, for our special benefit.

Knowledge was not a collective abstraction for Babbitt; it existed concretely and individually, wherever precept became example through the life and work of a sage. Each of us, he counselled, quoting Spinoza, should bear in mind an exemplar of human nature: *"idea hominis, tamquam naturae humanae exemplar."* The prototype to whom we invariably compared him, for reasons not far to seek, was Dr. Johnson. But it seems more deeply suggestive that the two portraits he placed in his Widener study were those of Sainte-Beuve and Charles Eliot Norton. Norton, who had been the friendliest among his teachers, incarnated the last refinement of an earlier Harvard, highly cultivated and many-minded yet somewhat amateurish and provincial. Given his friendship with Carlyle and Ruskin, or his services to archeology and the study of Dante, he has been rather superciliously evoked by George Santayana in a broadside attack on "the genteel tradition":

Old Harvard men will remember the sweet sadness of Professor Norton. He would tell his classes, shaking his head with a slight sigh, that the

Greeks did not play football. In America there had been no French cathedrals, no Venetian school of painting, no theater, and even no gentlemen, but only gentlemanly citizens.

Santayana's list of what was lacking reads like a parody of Henry James's famous lament on the flatness of the American scene; but the caricature makes clear, at any rate, why the role of the gentleman or *honnête homme* was so very strategic in Babbitt's thought. Though the rugged young Middle Westerner had no pretensions to the sort of gentility personified by the elderly Bostonian, still it was an attenuated link with the humanists of the Renaissance. What had been an elegiac reminiscence for Norton was transformed by Babbitt into a militant criterion. To implement it he turned more directly toward Europe, and toward a critical mentor as unlike the high-minded Norton as possible and no more like himself, the worldly and professional Sainte-Beuve. Babbitt was impressed by the penetrating psychology that could expertly sketch so vast a gallery of personalities; and his two principal courses in French literature were devoted to the writers Sainte-Beuve had studied at fullest length, Pascal and Chateaubriand. From Sainte-Beuve, too, Babbitt drew his method of exemplification through self-revealing passages. Sainte-Beuve is the veritable hero of Babbitt's most affirmative book, *The Masters of Modern French Criticism*, and is all but designated there as the universal doctor of the nineteenth century. But his range of sympathies, alas, is traceable to his century's lack of standards. Babbitt can accept his eclecticism, but not his relativism, when Sainte-Beuve confesses:

My curiosity, my desire to see everything, to look on everything at close quarters, my extreme pleasure at finding the relative truth of everything, involved me in this series of experiments, which have been for me only a long course in moral physiology.

And when he goes on to analyze and "botanize," professing himself "a naturalist of souls," he loses his American disciple. Babbitt returns intuitively to Norton's master, Emerson, who has redressed so many balances because he reconciles so many attitudes. The ideal critic, Babbitt decides, significantly noting that Sainte-Beuve's picture hung in Emerson's study at Concord, would combine the Frenchman's flexibility with the American's elevation.

III

RALPH WALDO EMERSON was a strikingly untraditional thinker; but his conception of the American scholar is by now a tradition in itself, to be saluted in passing on these occasions, and emulated all the more earnestly by outlanders migrating from the Middle West to New England. Babbitt, though descended from Plymouth colonists, had been born in 1865 at Dayton, Ohio. Though he was suspicious of the quest for origins, and too proud to welcome an intimate scrutiny of his background, it is always illuminating to find latent sources of inspiration more profound than the entries in a *curriculum vitae*. He was, it would seem, a chary correspondent; our archives have no document in his hand. Yet by a strangely ironic coincidence, which cannot embarrass his inherent dignity at this stage, we do possess two letters from his father. The first is addressed to Professor Henry W. Longfellow in 1847 from a youth of nineteen, who is teaching country school in Missouri, learning Spanish by himself, and anxious to study at Harvard. As a specimen of his potentialities, he submits two cantos of a would-be romantic poem, "Gem of the Sea." Longfellow need not have been impressed; the young poet did not get a scholarship; and he seems to have moved on in other directions. The second letter is dated from Los Angeles in 1898, when the writer was seventy and his unmentioned son was an instructor at Harvard. The recipient was Professor William James, whose approbation the elder Babbitt besought for his many discoveries and for a vaunted message to the world. This time his enclosure was part of a set of books titled *Human Culture and Cure*, replete with testimonials and illustrations, including a diagram of the author's brain.

Edwin Dwight Babbitt signed himself M.D.; but whether those initials stood for doctor of medicine or doctor of magnetism is uncertain; and that uncertainty may have awakened his son's skepticism about academic degrees. Dr. Babbitt, who could be consulted by mail, practised in the light of hypnotism, spiritualism, phrenology, clairvoyance, massages, sun-baths, electrical treatments, inhabited planets, and utopian socialism. He claimed to see bodily aura, and to have a consultant who saw atoms with the naked eye. As author, publisher, and bookseller, he brought out such items as *Babbitt's Health Guide, Vital Magnetism, the Fountain of Life*, and *Marriage, with Sexual and Social Up-Building*. Among the flyleaves he advertised such inventions as Psychomized Paper, the Chromo Disk, and the Grand Thermalume. But he remained what he had been, a teacher, managing a business school when Irving was a boy, and winding up in California as dean of an institution which styled itself the College of Fine Forces. Inasmuch as his advice to families was predicated upon "the innate nobility which every child possesses," this incorrigible reformer may have been a Wordsworthian — if not a Micawberish — parent. His own child grew up to harbor an intensive distrust of that assumption, together with a comprehensive disbelief in nature's remedies. William James, so bright and distant a luminary in the father's astral firmament, was the son's Cambridge neighbor and philosophical target; his *Varieties of Religious Experience* was tartly rechristened by Irving Babbitt as *Wild Religions I Have Known*. It may be that Babbitt's early exposure to pseudoscience at its wildest set his teeth on edge, and inoculated him against more substantial manifestations of the modern spirit.

Edwin Babbitt may have been a crackpot; but he was not a quack, since he so transparently believed in the schemes, contraptions, and panaceas he so volubly dispensed; and since his transcendental confidence does not seem to have been shared by the public, his enterprise did not even succeed materially in providing a stable home for his wife and five children. "Breaking up housekeeping" seems to have been their commonest childhood remembrance. Irving's mother died when he was eleven; though he was helped by uncles, he was soon on his own. During a sojourn in New York he sold papers; his incidental reference to newsboys and Negroes is by no means unfeeling. He worked on a farm in Ohio, a ranch in

Wyoming, and — as police reporter — a newspaper in Cincinnati. He had a varied acquaintance with American life before he graduated from high school, where he specialized in chemistry and civil engineering, to matriculate at college slightly older than his classmates, who considered him reserved and shy. To come to Harvard was not only to realize Edwin Babbitt's thwarted ambition; it was to recoil from the atmosphere of New Thought by embracing traditionalism. He concentrated in Classics, with high honors as a sophomore and plain honors on graduation in 1889, having incurred the displeasure of the Greek grammarian, William Watson Goodwin, through a belated composition. For the next two years, he taught Greek and Latin at the University of Montana. With his savings he fulfilled his plan of returning to Europe, where he had spent a strenuous junior year on a walking trip with a classmate; and in Paris, under Sylvain Lévi, he studied Sanscrit and Indian philosophy.

Notwithstanding these institutional associations, he had inherited from his self-taught father the autodidactic temperament. Avoiding the sanctioned routines by which *homo academicus* is moulded and rounded and polished, he lived the maxim that true education is self-education; and his educational goals were too far-reaching to fit within a departmental program. His formal training terminated with a master's degree from the Harvard Graduate School in 1893. Thence, after a year of teaching Romance Languages at Williams College, he gravitated back to the Harvard department, where for the next two decades his main assignments were undergraduate classes in the French language. Little by little he came to lecture in the interdepartmental field of Comparative Literature, taking over Lewis Gates's courses in the Romantic Movement and the History of Criticism, and introducing the course that became his uniquely personal vehicle: Rousseau and his Influence. Settled on Kirkland Road with a family of his own, his way of life could hardly have been more simple or methodical. Most of his social energies were held in reserve for the war of ideas he daily waged in the classroom. Accordingly, as one French visitor put it, he was "pedagogic in the drawing room." Though he was visiting professor for a term at the Sorbonne, he seldom resumed his European journeying. Having once seen the museums and cathedrals, a travelling companion reports, Babbitt preferred to read and write at his hotel. Nor could he ever be lured to the Orient, in spite of his lifelong interest in its culture and of Mrs. Babbitt's birth and upbringing in China. His orbit was Cambridge as Kant's had been Konigsberg. To accompany our peripatetic upon his local walks was, I may say, a vigorous exercise physically as well as intellectually.

Babbitt judged — and would have wanted others to judge him — by final causes, not beginnings but ends. His own end was an exemplary fulfillment of his belief in self-control, an enactment of Montaigne's adage that to philosophize is to learn how to die. His latter years were overshadowed by a wasting disease. Punctiliously he kept up with his academic responsibilities through the final examinations of 1933. Stoically he lingered on for five weeks as an invalid, setting his domestic affairs in order and working as much as he could on his translation of *The Dhammapada*. On one occasion, endeavoring to take his mind off the pain, Mrs. Babbitt suggested reading a detective story. This was a licensed indulgence for Paul Elmer More; but, as Babbitt may have remembered, it was also the esthetic passion of George Lyman Kittredge and the Philological Syndicate. Babbitt — who reread Homer in Greek for his own recreation — had characterized their specialistic researches as mere detective-work, and had alluded to John Livingston Lowes — his ablest antagonist in the battle over the Romantics — as "the most accomplished of literary sleuths." Hence, from his virtual deathbed, Babbitt rallied to answer his wife's suggestion firmly: "Detective stories? Good Lord, no! I can still meditate." The key to those ultimate thoughts was thought itself, unmitigated by anodynes. From his Buddhist text, to be posthumously published, he had translated:

Through meditation wisdom is won, through lack of meditation wisdom is lost; let a man who knows this double path of gain and loss so conduct himself that wisdom may grow.

The pervasive theme of *The Dhammapada* is the growth of wisdom as embodied in the earnest strivings of the wise man, the meditative Brahman who has attained the highest end, the leader not led by others who remains unshaken in the midst of praise or blame.

If you see an intelligent man who detects faults and blames what is blame-worthy, follow that wise man as though he were a revealer of (hidden) treasures.
Let him admonish, let him teach, let him forbid what is improper! — he will be beloved of the good, by the bad he will be hated.

All of us may secretly long for the guidance of such a sage, especially during our formative period, when we first seek it in the paternal image. Irving Babbitt must have been soon disappointed by the exemplar or *idea hominis* presented in Edwin Babbitt, whose pretensions formed an object-lesson in the need for common sense. It could be said of the son that he continued the father's examination of mental phenomena, dramatically forewarned of the tangents and heading straight for a center. It was a central path that brought Irving Babbitt to Harvard University. The elders he encountered there — Eliot and James, Goodwin and Kittredge — were models of sounder learning; yet he found them immersed in a *Zeitgeist* which had fostered the feckless tinkering he knew so well; they were specialized investigators rather than universal doctors; they were rather sleuths than sages. He liked to point out that the term "scholar" meant, etymologically speaking, a man of leisure; and the use of that leisure, he insisted, was not for revery but for reflection. The crown of meditation was mediation; scholarly contemplation should lead to action, which ought not to be confused with the hustling of committees. Babbitt's objective was the "spiritual strenuousness" of Buddha under the tree of perfect knowledge. Finding it unrealized elsewhere, he sought it through his own character and conviction. Gradually he became a guide for other seekers. From the East itself they came to Cambridge, as one Chinese scholar has recollected, "to sit at the feet of the new sage."

IV

BABBITT, according to More, was "greater as a teacher than a writer," and possibly greatest of all as a talker. His writing, often dictated to his wife, catches the firmness of his voice for those who heard it, though it misses the timing of his wit. Like other talkers, especially lecturers, he could be discursive and repetitious; but he held us by the richness of his anecdotal illustrations and epigrammatic comments; while he underscored his exposition, in Matthew Arnold's manner, with telling catchwords. Babbitt's seven books, largely based upon his lectures and articles, are integrated through his underlying preoccupations. Their emphasis ranges from esthetics to politics via philosophy. Their pattern is varied by the endless mosaic of apophthegms and instances. The hidden treasures they reveal are nothing more nor less than the great commonplaces, which have been made increasingly uncommon by the novelties of material progress. The extracts that Babbitt prescribes are drawn from the distillations of human experience. The authorities whom he cites, approached as a body, constitute that very principle of authority which he invokes. This testament of wisdom is not limited to the western hemisphere, grand as the Greco-Roman tradition of *paideia* has been; one of Babbitt's most far-sighted contributions was his insistence that an enlightened world-view must come to terms with Asiatic thought. Nor was he, in his running critique of "a cheap contemporaneousness," an uncritical praiser of the ancients; he described himself as "a modern of moderns," though decidedly not a modernist, yet a thoroughgoing individualist; and, in describing his philosophical outlook, he employed such words as "positive," "empirical," and even "experimental." His whole endeavor with the past was to make it live in the present, to learn and teach the lessons of history.

Babbitt took his educational stand in that slowly ripened first book of his, *Literature and the American College: Essays in Defense of the Humanities.* His opening chapter, "What is Humanism?," propounded a question he had raised as early as 1895, in a

17

guest lecture at the University of Wisconsin, and would pursue to
the point where it instigated a public controversy thirty-five years
afterward. His epigraph was a passage from Emerson, which he
found many further occasions to quote, distinguishing between two
irreconcilable laws: "Law for man, and law for thing." It was the
age-old distinction recognized by the Greeks between νόμος and
φύσις, custom and nature. The consequences of flouting it have
been labelled by sociologists as *anomie*, and are somewhat more
humanely set forth by the Emersonian poet, Robert Frost:

> As long on earth
> As our comparisons were stoutly upward
> With gods and angels, we were men at least,
> But little lower than the gods and angels.
> But once comparisons were yielded downward,
> Once we began to see our images
> Reflected in the mud and even dust,
> 'Twas disillusion upon disillusion.
> We were lost piecemeal to the animals,
> Like people thrown out to delay the wolves.

Thus the human condition may be located midway in the hierarchy
of being, whence it may look upward toward the supernatural or
downward toward the naturalistic level. The humanism of the
Renaissance, prompted by the rediscovery of the classics, rescued
man from the dizzying aspirations and rarefied altitudes of medieval
theology. But his descent did not stop at the half-way house where
he was most at home, in Babbitt's interpretation; it went on by
reducing civilization to the plane of things and animals. Existence
was traced, by philosophers like Bergson, to a vital urge from the
depths of the unconscious, *élan vital*. Babbitt would have centered
the process on a *frein vital* — or, to repeat the phrase he borrowed
from Emerson, who had borrowed the notion from his oriental
reading, an "inner check." The moral issue was whether the intri-
cate compound of human nature should be dominated by its human
or by its natural component. The tendency toward dehumanization,
for Babbitt, coincided historically with the Romantic Movement.
Romanticism, as he redefined it, was the Pandora's box that had

released all the other isms to harass our world — beginning with humanitarianism, which he considered a travesty of humanism. The most persuasive ideologue of the movement, Jean-Jacques Rousseau, was Babbitt's personal devil. That omnipresent role was warranted by the scope of Rousseau's influence, if not by Babbitt's own habit of pointing out awful examples. Rousseau exemplified the sentimentalist, whose cultivation and exhibition of impulse had undermined the strict self-discipline of the sages, revolutionizing for the worst the *idea hominis*.

This was a situation, not a doctrine, as Ramon Fernandez could observe from a distance. The diagnosis was acute enough, though the prescription becomes more problematic. Babbitt was fundamentally a moralist, like the Existentialists of today; like them, he sought a metaphysical groundwork for his ethics. But, as his Swedish expositor, Folke Leander, concludes: "For Babbitt the epistemological problem . . . finally runs into the ethical problem." So, we should add, does every other problem. His concept of an inner check, or higher will, approximates what Protestants would call conscience and Freudians would term the superego. Some of his fellow travellers travelled farther than he, notably More and T. S. Eliot, in coming to believe that the ethical problem could be solved only by adopting a religious position. They confronted Babbitt with a dilemma: to be either a naturalist or a supernaturalist, either to ally himself with the enemy or to join his allies on a pilgrimage to Canterbury or Rome. Here was no excluded middle for him; rather, it was the central span of his dualism; and he did not need the shelter of dogma to keep his metaphysics warm. Like Sainte-Beuve, he could emerge with respect and regret from the vanished spiritual retreat of Port-Royal. "Speaking . . . not as an orthodox Christian but simply as a psychological observer," Babbitt was keenly interested in Christianity, utterly fascinated by Buddhism, and probably most sympathetic to the secular creed of Confucius. "Professor Babbitt knows too much," wrote Mr. Eliot frankly — too much about comparative religion to be converted by particular articles of faith. He remained the self-reliant individualist, who — with Vigny's isolated thinker — might have professed: *"Le vrai Dieu, le Dieu fort, est le Dieu des idées!"* The humanist, as a skeptic yet not an agnostic, would pay equal attention to both lines of Pope's well-balanced couplet:

> Know then thyself, presume not God to scan,
> The proper study of mankind is man.

Facing the dilemma's other horn, naturalism, an unimpaled Babbitt made common cause with Anglo-Catholics, Neo-Thomists, and other religionists, as well as skeptical traditionalists. The real gulf was the one that yawned like Pascal's, whenever communication was attempted between the academic world and contemporary letters. When Babbitt's energetic disciple, Stuart P. Sherman, resigned from his professorship of English at the University of Illinois to become editor of the *New York Herald-Tribune's* weekly book-review, his old teacher told him he was trying to build a bridge between Irving and George F. Babbitt. Sherman died all too prematurely; yet during the later Twenties the catchphrase "New Humanism," was more and more in the air; and Babbitt's increasingly vocal disciples acquired a monthly organ, *The Bookman*. Finally, on May 9, 1930, the master himself "invaded New York, the stronghold of his enemies," — to echo the patriotic account in the *New York Times* — and submitted his views to a debate with Carl Van Doren and Henry Seidel Canby. Symbolically, the amplifiers at Carnegie Hall broke down; but it is clear that Babbitt was his intransigent self, and that the audience overwhelmingly favored his easy-going antagonists. "Though it was a very warm day," Babbitt conceded, back in Cambridge, "the occasion might be described as a frost." Yet the *Kulturkampf* raged on in the periodicals, reaching its climax that same year when the quasi-official symposium, *Humanism and America*, provoked a counterattack from dissenting critics, *The Critique of Humanism*. The latter, we must admit, was the livelier volume: Edmund Wilson carried the battle of books into Babbitt's camp by accusing him of turning Sophocles into "a Harvard humanist." However, there was no genuine meeting of minds. The Humanists argued for a timeless ethic, the free-lances for a timely esthetic — neither successfully, as it turned out.

That discussion ushered in the Thirties, with their prevailing trend toward social criticism. Insofar as this called for moral commitment, Neo-Humanism may have prepared the way. The New Marxism was hardly the Great Awakening preached by the professorial doctrinaires. But Babbitt had consistently warned them against expecting their kind of revival; once humanism was taken up as a fad, it was bound to go the way of all isms. He was glad to see it revert to the Academy, where its continuing function is to transcend the ephemeral. The date of his death was so pivotal that, in retrospect, we cannot wish he had survived it; for 1933 brought a wave of authoritarianism which caught up some of his more reactionary followers. Babbitt had expressed discomfort over the political extremism of his French *confrères* associated with the Action Française; and in *Democracy and Leadership* he criticized American society from the reasonable vantage-point of Burke's independent conservatism. Like most of our respectable conservatives, he thought of himself as a genuine liberal. Never professing to be wholly orthodox, he could not apply the stigma of heresy to his opponents, as the more fanatical have subsequently done. Temperamentally, Stuart Sherman remarked, he may have been a radical out of his time. Had he been born into a classical age, Austin Warren suggests, he might have opposed its orthodoxy: "was not his real role that of adversary?" If we seek Mr. Eliot's detached opinion, we might turn to that infernal passage where the poet encounters the spirit of "some dead master," who tells him:

> I am not eager to rehearse
> My thought and theory which you have forgotten.
> These things have served their purpose: let them be . . .
> For last year's words belong to last year's language
> And next year's words await another voice.

Our climate has so changed in the last generation that it seems vain to interrogate the dead. And it is with private relief that I refrain from asking Sainte-Beuve's question: what would our predecessors have thought of us? The situations Babbitt deplored have, in some respects, been aggravated. Commercialization has flourished; standardization has certainly not decreased; menacing techniques of popular manipulation have been devised. Culture itself is projected and interconnected through networks infinitely more efficient and powerful than the system of amplification that failed in 1930 at Carnegie Hall; we are more dependent than ever on gadgets and slogans, more estranged from "a sense of the inner life." Our spokesmen still take that "quantitative view of life" which Babbitt reprehended, and the quantities may have affected the qualities for the worse. We live in a world of science fiction come true, where George F. Babbitt may bask in a Grand Thermalume; where Edwin Babbitt, with his Vital Magnetism, might seem less of a crank than Irving Babbitt, with his Inner Check. Law for Thing has provided utilitarianism with an unanswerable argument in the shape of a mushroom cloud. The ideal of the Gentlemen seems hopelessly outmoded, at a moment when the prime qualification for our highest office — so millions are reported to feel — is the ability to talk back to Premier Khrushchev. Babbitt's censure may indeed be more pertinent than ever before. But we pay him small tribute by echoing his formulas. We should do much better by emulating the moral courage he showed in withstanding the drift of circumstances.

V

IT is the merit of the innovator, which Babbitt wryly granted Rousseau, to ask the right questions though he may give the wrong answers. It is the merit of the traditionalist to give the right answers to questions no longer moot, which ought nonetheless to be reconsidered and more broadly reformulated. Thus Babbitt's approach to the cultural crisis of modernity was adapted from Arnold's, and Arnold had already been conducting a rear-guard defense of a waning tradition. Culture — for both critics — was a certain type of education, admittedly the best, and nearly everything else was anarchy. But culture, so defined, has meanwhile almost withered away; while anarchy, in need of redefinition, has organized itself and set up vast subcultures of its own. Babbitt, more than fifty years ago, could refer nostalgically to "the almost lost art of reading." He could not have foreseen a technological revolution, no less consequential than the development of the printed book which it may now be supplanting with audio-visual media. Yet he had taken issue with the Romanticists because he feared their hostility to book-learning. Wordsworth had dismissed "those barren leaves" in favor of nature's greenery and the "spontaneous wisdom" of the wood, which — he maintained in "The Tables Turned" — could teach us so much more than "the meddling intellect" of "all the sages." Therein the poet was answering his friend, whose more traditional attitude had been stated at the outset of the preceding poem, "Expostulation and Reply." It might be said of Babbitt that he turned the tables back again, and that his life-work was an expostulation against the Romantic reply to the neo-classicists. Man was not born yesterday, after all; but our forebears will have lived in vain unless we take advantage of their bequest, which is the sole guarantee of our children's enlightenment.

> "Where are your books? — that light bequeathed
> To Beings else forlorn and blind?
> Up! up! and drink the spirit breathed
> From dead men to their kind.
>
> "You look round on your Mother Earth,
> As if she for no purpose bore you;
> As if you were her first-born birth,
> And none had lived before you!"

In America, the land of innovation, there have been pragmatic reasons for scanning the horizon so naively. There has also been, on the part of an augmenting minority, keen awareness of tradition. Emerson's alignment, the party of hope, has always won the majorities in its intermittent dialectic with the party of memory. Consequently the task of the adversary has become all the more urgently needful and useful. Babbitt was sometimes accused of being a destructive critic, who ignored beauties in order to stigmatize faults;

and it is true, to adopt his quizzical expression, that his gustos were less memorable than his disgustos. His library was crammed with such unexpected authors as André Gide, whose pages were not merely cut and thumbed but crisply underlined and emphatically annotated. To whatever came his way, Babbitt's response was whole-heartedly critical, generally involving a conflict of principle and tending more often than not toward an adverse judgment. To blame what was blameworthy, he believed, was the only means of maturely resisting our national disposition to be "childishly un-critical." Where the Everlasting Yea had too many partisans, and the Spirit of Denial all too few, the man of moral stature would be he who — as Melville wrote — says no in thunder, though the devil bids him say yes. Babbitt's dissidence had made him apt at framing military metaphors, especially in scholastic contexts. When some of us told him that we had invited John Dewey to address the Harvard Classical Club, his mock-heroic comment was: "You have let the enemy into the citadel." After that alert, it was slightly anticlimac-tic when Dewey read us an unexceptionably conventional paper about the Pre-Socratics; but it may have foreshadowed the dialectical process that is now leading our educators up, up from the pastures of permissiveness and back toward the citadels of discipline.

Babbitt might himself have become a classical scholar, had not his undergraduate experience discouraged him, and had he not been temperamentally inclined to polemic rather than apologia. In his negatively humorous moods, he deprecated his own subject, French, as "a cheap and nasty substitute for Latin." More positively and seriously, he regarded France as the center of modern civilization, on the particular grounds that criticism was so express and charac-teristic a trait of its literature. Yet as he declared in his preface to *The New Laokoon*, it was "one-sided" to study "one literature"; an acquaintance with several, in their interrelationship, was prerequisite for any understanding of genres and movements; indeed Rousseau had attained his peculiar predominance through what Joseph Texte, the first official French *comparatiste*, has termed "literary cosmopoli-tanism." Hence Babbitt was instrumental in efforts to humanize the college curriculum by establishing an honors program in Classics and Allied Subjects, and by examining students of Modern Languages in the Bible, Shakespeare, and Ancient Authors. Given his interests and abilities, it was inevitable that he become identified with Comparative Literature. Not so much a field as a perspective, our subject — or rather, our object — owes its existence to the pooled resources of various departments, contributed with a magnanimity which — I hope — will continue to be perennial. At Harvard, professors have offered courses in Comparative Literature since 1892; since 1904 there has been a department offering graduate degrees. Understandably, the original focus was upon the vernacular literatures of the Middle Ages. Babbitt enlarged it to comprehend the prospect opened up by Arnold in his inaugural lecture of 1857 at Oxford:

. . . everywhere there is connection, everywhere there is illustration; no single event, no single literature, is adequately comprehended except in its relation to other events, to other literatures. The literature of ancient Greece, the literature of the Christian Middle Age, so long as they are regarded as two isolated literatures, two isolated growths of the human spirit, are not adequately comprehended; and it is adequate comprehension which is the demand of the present age.

This vision of cultural relatedness, of an intellectual continuum extending through time and space, beckons us toward that realm of Goethe's promise, *Weltliteratur*. In a world which strains at the boundaries of nationalism, why should they be perpetuated by literature, which has crossed them so freely in the past? Arnold moves on by quoting Prince Albert, whose choice of words inadvertently helps to strengthen the meaning of our problematic term, "comparative":

"We must compare," — the illustrious Chancellor of Cambridge said the other day to his hearers at Manchester, — "we must compare the works of other ages with those of our own age and country; that, while we feel proud of the immense development of knowledge and power of production which we possess, we may learn humility in contemplating the refinement of feeling and intensity of thought manifested in the works of the older schools."

25

Verily, the study of Comparative Literature should inculcate the lesson of humility. Given the limitations that languages sooner or later lay down, no one would presume to take all of letters for his province; one simply tries to counteract one's innate provinciality, and to obtain a more objective view of what one may know, by relevant comparisons with whatever one can learn. To be a humanist, alas, has come to mean little more than not to be a scientist, and occasionally to defend one's interests by attacking those of one's colleagues. Meanwhile the humanities, like the sciences, have perforce been chopped up and thrown to the specialists, though there is an observable reaction in favor of Babbitt's catholicity. On the other hand, the scientific viewpoint has been broadened and chastened to an extent which may outdate some of his reservations. Faced with the dilemma between naturalism and supernaturalism, those who cannot embrace a supernatural credo — as he could not — may find their working solution in a concept of nature tempered by humanity: of Law for Man refining on Law for Thing, which it is man's privilege to comprehend, if not altogether to control. A naturalist, so long as he is preoccupied with souls, can still be humane. If there is a distribution of academic labor between "the two cultures," there should be — as C. P. Snow has lately argued — a sharing of intellectual responsibility. To what has proved an unproductive debate, President Eliot may well be allowed the last word: "This University recognizes no real antagonism between literature and science." Each of them has too much to learn from the other.

Much has been happening within the sphere of literary studies, however delimited. The locution "creative," which used to make Babbitt wince, has become the staple of English Departments, where it designates a mode of writing that is virtually neo-classical in its dependence on imitation. The chronological emphasis has shifted all the way from the medieval to the modern period: from one extreme of unripeness to another, in Babbitt's estimation. Though he broke down barriers between criticism and scholarship, we cannot imagine him hailing a revival of criticism unsupported by scholarship. J. E. Spingarn, the one contemporary whose achievement might have been comparable, if his scholarly career had not been interrupted, clashed with Babbitt over esthetics and called for a "New Criticism." That call was answered by a later generation of teacher-critics, many of them tradition-conscious Southerners, whose cardinal virtue was Babbitt's chief deficiency, a concern with form. Babbitt's main concern had been explicit in the title of his Dartmouth address, "On Teaching the Intellectual Content of Literature"; and it seems appropriate that he wrote a pamphlet on French writers for the introductory series entitled "Reading with a Purpose." Reading for pleasure, and with a perceptive eye for stylistic effect, was undeniably subordinated to the more austere demands of humanistic pedagogy. Nowadays the pendulum of taste has swung so far in the formalistic direction that such purposefulness is apt to be condemned as heretical or fallacious. Yet a narrowly rhetorical method is no more conducive to rounded estimates than what has come to be known as content-analysis. Babbitt had taken the opposite course in reaction from belletristic colleagues, whose appreciation of books — as he lamented in his Twenty-Five-Year Class Report — was "insufficiently vivified by ideas." Style, he reflected in a last address to the American Academy of Arts and Letters, "bears a relation to one's total outlook on life." Even John Keats, after all, when pausing in contemplation before a certain well-wrought urn, permitted himself to speculate about the lives and thoughts of the youths and maidens depicted thereon. Beauty is not invariably truth, and it is for the critic to press the distinction. To be truly positive and empirical, he must bring historical consciousness to his formal analysis; his understanding of the text must be grounded in its context of signification.

If newer critics have narrowed their scope and lowered their sights, we now have a broader category for what Babbitt practised, in the grand manner of Arnold's criticism of life or the *politiques et moralistes* of nineteenth-century France. His terrain, which bordered on so many others, was basically the history of ideas, the middle ground between literature and philosophy. In cultivating it, he was less dispassionate or systematic than the professional philosopher, Arthur Lovejoy, with whom he engaged in a stimulating controversy. It was, in fact, Babbitt's passionate sense of involvement which enabled him to reanimate the play of intellectual forces so vividly and concretely. Romanticism was the causal nexus explaining the modern epoch, to him and his students, because it had captured men's minds and altered their values on an unprecedented scale. From his standpoint, it had blurred clear and distinct ideas into confusing and seductive images. Those who responded more sympathetically rejected his strictures as unimaginative; yet it was the power of imagination which preoccupied him beyond all other themes; and he frequently recurred to Pascal's insight that "the imagination disposes of everything," or to Napoleon's acknowledgment that "imagination rules the world." At a date when historians stressed material factors and leaned heavily upon economic determinism, Babbitt's belief that man should be master of things must have seemed quixotically bookish. But the subsequent rise of revolutionary Communism has demonstrated, contrary to the implications of Marx's own dialectical materialism, that Law for Thing can be overmastered by ideology. The idea itself, in the struggle for man's future, will be a more potent weapon than the atom or the dollar. Against the mounting pressures that encroach from all sides upon the autonomy of the individual, the single stratagem Babbitt would recommend is to exercise "the ethical imagination": the will to resist what seems evil in the name of what seems good. As for the delicate and difficult matter of judging between them, what, if not Law for Man, can teach us that ultimate mode of discrimination? And where should we be looking for it, if not at the very heart of the educational process?

CPSIA information can be obtained
at www.ICGtesting.com
Printed in the USA
BVHW01s2350040218
507224BV00009B/107/P